Fun Meals
for
Fathers and Sons

Recipes and Activities
for
Bonding and Mentoring

by Akili Kumasi
with Asiedu & Netfa Heywot-Kumasi

LOVE
GOD IS LOVE

GIL PUBLICATIONS
P. O. Box 80275
Brooklyn, NY 11208
www.GILpublications.com

Fun Meals for Fathers and Sons
Recipes and Activities
For Bonding and Mentoring

by Akili Kumasi
with Asiedu & Netfa Heywot-Kumasi

ISBN: 0-9626035-1-1
ISBN 13: 978-0-9626035-1-8

Copyright © 2004 by GIL Publications
A division of The God Is Love Ministries

For information please contact:

GIL PUBLICATIONS
P. O. Box 80275
Brooklyn, NY 11208
www.GILpublications.com
info@GILpublications.com

Dedication

Fun Meals for Fathers and Sons is dedicated to the Father and Son who without them - this book would not be possible, that is God the Father and God the Son.

> "All things have been committed to me by my
> Father. No one knows the Son except the Father,
> and no one knows the Father except the Son...."
> Matthew 11:27 (NIV)

Table of Contents

Introduction

Fun Meals for Fathers and Sons has evolved from a very special moment in our kitchen into a full blown recipe for male bonding and mentoring. One day my sons and I were in the kitchen talking. I was cooking and they were drawing and enjoying our time together. We were talking about all the special meals that I make for them. Next we started making a list and the book idea naturally flowed from there. I dictated the recipes to Asiedu and Netfa started typing them on the computer.

As we wrote down the recipes we realized that our meals are not just "things" to eat. They are "experiences" to have. We designed the recipes and activities with both fathers and sons in mind. The idea is to get everyone involved as much as possible in all aspects of the meals thus creating an atmosphere for sharing and learning. There's another point here as well - and that is to just have fun - enjoying each other.

This book is intended to help the bonding process between boys and their fathers which is so important in this day and age. Helping men to be involved in their sons' lives, providing direction, being a role model, and just sharing positive male energy is our goal. There is no slight intended to daughters and mothers as all of the meals and activities can be done by - and with - mothers and daughters. But, I do have a particular interest in help fathers help their sons to also become good men. The recipes and activities in this book are also good for grandfathers, uncles, step-fathers and older brothers to bond with younger males.

All the recipes are very simple and easy to make. You don't have to be a gourmet chef to prepare these meals. In fact, you might already know how to make some of these meals, but the point here is not always to give you something that you do not already know. We want to - in a time of need - give you some food for thought – (sorry about the pun) - that could help you create a special activity.

Fun Meals for Fathers and Sons has two sections: the first section is a series of recipes for meals and the second is a series of activities that are centered around meals. Both sections provide recipes for fun, adventure and excitement that helps in the bonding process for boys and their fathers.

Recipes for Fathers and Sons

We suggest that the children be as involved as possible in all stages of the meal. Many recipes provide suggestions for how to get the children involved in different aspects:

1) Plan the meal together (when possible). Sometimes making it a surprise is also a winner. Use the following questions as guides for planning a meal.

   What are you going to have? How is it going to be prepared or cooked? Who is going to do what?

2) Shopping

   What items are you going to need from the store? Make a list together. Go together to get the items on the list. This is a great opportunity for lessons in economics.

3) Preparation and Cooking

   You can get the children involved in ways that are not dangerous - especially for young children. Doing it together can bring a special level of satisfaction and a sense of accomplishment.

4) Eat the meals together

With some meals we have a special way of eating or serving the meal. Create your own fun – and traditions.

5) Clean-Up

This is always a joint effort!

Activities for Fathers and Sons

The activities section of the book is also very exciting. There are suggestions for numerous activities. Most of the meals are for away from home. Some are for at the home. All of them are centered around a meal but can be done with your own creativity. We do a lot of these activities as we are always making something special out of something ordinary. These activities can become your special activities and your children will look forward to them.

My sons and I worked on this book off-and-on for almost five years. We continued to add artwork, recipes and activities to our collection. We find that as we do things over and over - we change them. This is the best way to benefit from this book. Use your own ideas and creativity when trying our recipes and activities.

Your children can also learn a lot about cooking through this experience. When they get out on their own they can actually cook for themselves instead of relying on non-nutritional fast foods.

We know that many of you have your own ideas about fun meals that you already do and many of you will create new ideas as you try our recipes and activities. Send us your recipes and activities. We will publish the most unique ones in the second volume of *Fun Meals*. See the back section of this book for details.

Creating *Fun Meals for Fathers and Sons* has been quite an experience. We certainly hope you enjoy it!

Akili Kumasi

Bonding and Mentoring

"For years we have known that youth learn to have good interpersonal relationships from their encounters at the dinner table in their homes. The dinner hour is one of the most important hours in a child's life. It's the hour that is made for listening, as well as sharing the hurts, pains, victories, and blessings of the day. It is a time for learning to communicate." These words of wisdom from Dr. Ed Cole's *Maximized ManHood*[1] embody the spirit of this book. *Fun Meals for Fathers and Sons* expands on this concept and takes meals to another level.

With the meals and activities in *Fun Meals for Fathers and Sons* dining becomes an adventure. In the process, relationships can be built and maintained.

The primary objective of being a father is the raising of your children and helping them to secure a promising future free from the entrapments that plague our society today. Your role as the male parent in their life is crucial.

The higher the level of ManHood we demand from ourselves means the higher the level of standards we impress on our sons.

The Bible says in Proverb 22:6 (NIV), "Train a child in the way he should go, and when he is old he will not turn from it." Most parents know this principle without having to quote it. However, some of us have difficulty reaching our children. Others, who may not be having difficulty, don't want to get to the point where they do have difficulties reaching their children.

This is why bonding and mentoring is so important. In today's society we need to be close to our sons in a positive way so

---

[1]   Edwin Louis Cole, Maximized ManHood: A Guide to Family Survival, (Springdale, PA: Whitaker House, 1982) p. 140-41.

we don't lose them to all the non-sense that's pulling at their attention.

The activities and meals in *Fun Meals for Fathers and Sons* can help to create the atmosphere for continuous bonding that helps insure that we will always be close to our children. With these meals and activities my sons and I have already created "traditions" we each look forward to. We have etched good memories that can never be replaced. We've shared ourselves with each other in a way that lends itself to open communication.

Bonding is ever so important to the communication process. And communication is one of the most important elements in any relationship. By bonding with my sons over some silly meals I am able to tell them stories and get them in a mood where they hear me completely - and they respond with their own thoughts, feelings, insights and questions. They've even told me - more than once - that I should write a book about some of the things I have taught them about life.

It's important to hug your children and laugh with them - and it's a lot easier to do with a mouth full of roasted marshmallows or while your child is intently working at the stove over a pot of ground meat and taco mix.

There is great satisfaction when one of my sons creates a meal he wants; we design it; we shop together for the ingredients and then we fix it. The result: I've got a satisfied young man on my hands. He feels heard, loved and fulfilled. He has a sense of accomplishment - and so do I. Now he's open to talk with me and listen to me because I've shown trust in him. Now he can trust me. I can begin mentoring on a serious level - expounding principles and ideas to his young mind. I can talk about the rigors, responsibilities and rewards of being a man. This type of ManHood Training is most effective on an informal basis - when it's heartfelt and spontaneous.

Let's face it - we have fathers out there that don't have a clue and need help. We also have fathers who are doing a good job and have something they can share with others. We also have fathers who are trying their hardest and are having a very rough time. We come in all spectrums, sizes, shapes and colors. But we are all in this together because it is our sons who will be running this country in just a few short decades. What we do for them now will help determine whether they are making a positive contribution to society, living a happy life or struggling to make ends meet or stay out of jail.

Whatever your situation, most of us want our children to have better than what we had. We want to give them the benefit of our knowledge and experience. It is our job to make sure we have the type of relationship with our sons (and daughters) that affords us the opportunity to hear from them what is going on in their young lives, to know their feelings, trials, tribulations and successes - and to impart our experiential knowledge and wisdom. Having fun and food together helps in building these kinds of relationship.

This book is also a great tool for the divorced or separated father who does not live with his children. Do you know how important it is to your child that you come to pick them up, spend time with them, tell them and show them that they are special to you. Your children may not show you, or tell you, but believe me it matters a great deal. You must be consistent - and on time. How you treat your children who are separated from you is critical to the development of their self-esteem - which in turn has great impact on their lives and the decisions they make throughout their lives. Having special meals that you and your children can create together at your house is a winner for your children. It gives them something to look forward to. It can also get you off the hook if you aren't sure what to do with them. It's cheaper than amusement parks and means a whole lot more in the long run and the short-term.

Fun Meals for Fathers and Sons lends itself to your own creativity as well. It's a starting point if you are not sure what to do. Get them involved. This books provides a lot of "food for thought" (there's that pun again) about how to get something going with them on a Saturday when you know you should be spending time with them but you don't know what to do. Get busy. Create your own meals and your own traditions.

And fathers, after you've created some new memories, send us a note telling us about your successes with the meals and the moments. My sons and I will test your recipes and publish them in a new book - Volume Two of *Fun Meals*. Please see the announcement at the back of this book.

Show your sons (and daughters) some love openly. Give them a hug. Kiss them on the top of their head - whatever works. It's probably no problem for you to scold them or correct them in public. Try public praise and private discipline. The more you show them love the more they will show you love. Break down that facade of machoism. Have a *Fun Meal* and get the ball rolling!

Akili Kumasi

Cooking Utensils

POT

SKILLET

COOKING
SPOON

COOKING
FORK

SPATULA

COOKIE SHEET

KNIFE

Eating Utensils

FORK

KNIFE

DRNKNG
GLASS

SPOON

BOWL

PLATE

SAUCER

Breakfast Recipes

Rail Road Eggs

Railroad Eggs is a full and fancy breakfast that I learned when I was about 7 years old from my baby-sitter's husband. He was a cook on the railroad in his youth and he had a host of uniquely creative dishes. The name Railroad Eggs comes from how the bacon looks on the fried eggs. It resembles a set of railroad tracks. The bacon is right in the eggs.

Ingredients

- eggs
- bacon
- cooking oil

Directions

First, cook the bacon in long crisp stripes in a skillet. Next - after the bacon is cooked and strained on paper towels - the eggs will be fried (its okay if the yoke breaks). Warm up the oil in the frying pan to cook the eggs. Crack open two eggs into the center of the frying pan and immediately place two stripes of bacon parallel on top of the eggs.

When its time to turn the eggs over the bacon should stay right on the eggs. When finished, turn the eggs back over and you have railroad tracks of bacon on your eggs.

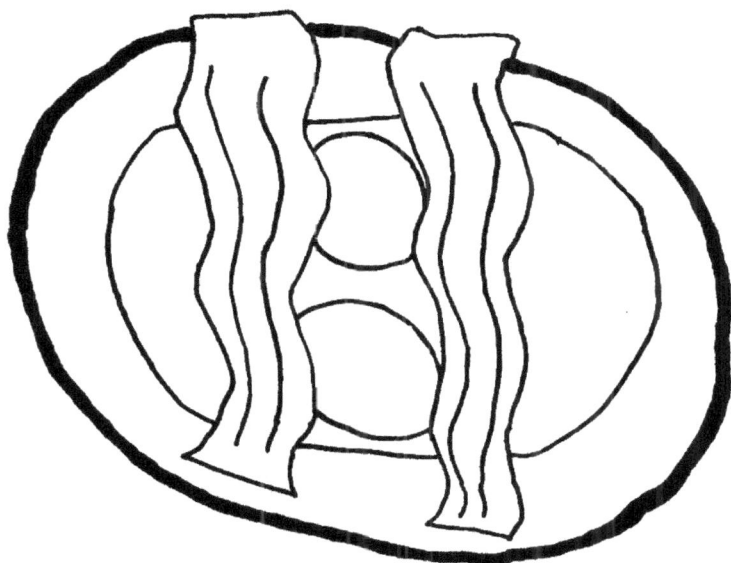

Serve with toast, potatoes, juice and love.

Eggs and Cheese on Toast

Eggs and Cheese on Toast in an excellent meal when you are on the run. It goes well in the car on the way to the camping trip or a day out at the beach, park or museum. Simply make the sandwich, wrap it in foil and be on your way.

If you're not on the run it can provide a good opportunity to teach your young one how to cook by letting them crack open and then scramble the eggs. When they are old enough and tall enough they can actually cook the eggs on the stove. Either way, they surely can put the bread in the toaster and butter it when it comes out of the toaster.

Ingredients

- eggs
- cheese
- bread
- butter
- cooking oil

This sandwich can also be made with meat. Add bacon, ham or sausage. For those of us who don't eat pork - you can get turkey or beef bacon, turkey ham, turkey sausage or even vegetable sausage.

Directions

First you get everything ready - then you cook.

Crack open the eggs into a bowl. Scramble the eggs in the bowl, season with pepper. Get the bread out for all the sandwiches. Slice or separate the sliced cheese. Heat (not to high) the frying pan with a little oil (one tablespoon per two eggs).

Start the toast - butter immediately after it comes out of toaster. Cook the eggs in the frying pan - continuously scramble them once they start to cook.

When eggs are finished put the eggs and cheese on the toast. Wrap in foil if you are traveling or just put them on plates and serve.

Another option, if you are staying home, is to put all the finished ingredients on each person's plate and let them construct their own sandwich.

Grilled CornBread Muffins and Syrup

Grilled Cornbread Muffins and Syrup is one of those breakfasts that was created out of necessity. It went over with a big bang.

There I was one morning without breakfast supplies but with some leftover muffins from the previous night's dinner. Enter a knife, a little butter and there you have it: Grilled Cornbread Muffins. It was so good that I started buying cornbread muffins just to grill for breakfast.

Ingredients

- cornbread muffins
- butter or margarine
- syrup, honey or jelly

Directions

Remember: the children can do a lot of the prep work and you do the cooking if they are not old enough. Safety first! Cut the CornBread Muffins in half. Spread a little butter on each half of the cornbread muffin. Heat frying pan on medium fire. Place buttered muffins (buttered side down) in the frying pan. Let them brown for about 5-6 minutes; turn over as desired.

Serve with syrup, honey or jelly as a topping. Goes great with scrambled eggs.

Waffles and Bacon Sandwich

A Waffles and Bacon Sandwich is a breakfast delight. It is similar to Pigs in blanket. Let the children make the sandwiches for themselves.

Ingredients

- waffles
- bacon, ham or sausage

Directions

Cook the bacon, ham or sausage.

Cook the waffles. You can cook waffles from scratch or use frozen waffles. With the frozen waffles all you have to do is pop them in the toaster, microwave oven or warm them on a cookie sheet in the oven.

After cooked, butter the waffles.

Place the bacon, ham or sausage between two waffles, cut them, pour syrup and eat.

Chicken and Waffles

Chicken and Waffles is one of the tastiest and most satisfying breakfasts a child and father can have. You can also have this for lunch or dinner if you want. It can all be made from scratch or frozen pre-fab foods. The chicken can even be gotten from your favorite take-out restaurant. Either way its a king's delight. This meal is great for a Sunday morning feast, late breakfast or brunch in front of the T.V. for football, cartoons or classic kid's movie.

Ingredients

- chicken
- waffles
- syrup
- butter

Directions

This meal is described in its simplest form. If you want to make everything from scratch go right ahead - you'll spend more time in the kitchen and less time in the feast. (If you choose to make everything see the directions for the fried chicken in the dinner section of this book.)

On the night before, child and father should take a trip to the grocery store with the list in hand. From the frozen section you want to pick up the fried chicken and waffles. Make sure you get enough for seconds, thirds and for anyone else who might just happen to join in with you.

Season the chicken with a little garlic powder, paprika and pepper - if desired, pop it into the oven or microwave according to the directions on the box. Next: cook the waffles according to the directions on the box in the toaster, oven or microwave. Keep in mind that these directions are usually simple enough for a school age child to read them to the father.

The best place to feast on this meal is on the coffee table or portable trays in front of the T.V. while watching a fantasy or adventure movie.

While the food is cooking, prepare the space where you will eat with all the necessities like utensils, drinks, syrup etc.

Have some popcorn ready for near the end of the movie. See Popcorn and OJ in the snacks section of this book.

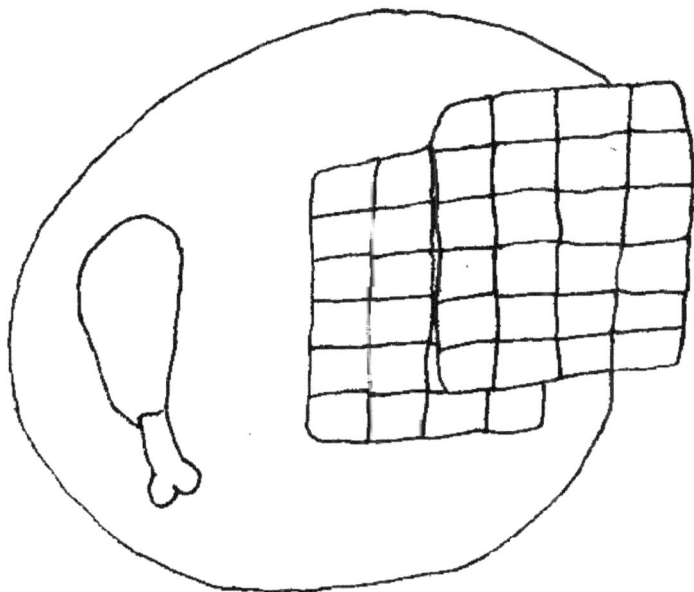

Bacon, Tator Tots®
and Ketchup

Bacon, Tator Tots and Ketchup is easy and fun. It's a little different from a traditional breakfast - but an easy one to get the children involved in.

Ingredients

- 4 strips of bacon for each person (turkey, beef or pork)
- 12-15 tator tots each

Directions

Bacon:

While the tator tots are cooking lay the bacon strips in a skillet. Cook until done. Place cooked bacon on paper towels to strain.

Tator Tots:

Pre-heat the oven according to the directions on the tator tots package (usually about ten minutes).

Let the children spread the tator tots on a cookie sheet - season lightly with garlic powder, paprika and pepper.
Cook for the appropriate amount of time.

This meal goes well with scrambled eggs, juice or sliced fruit.

I happen to like a little mustard mixed in with my ketchup but my boys like it with only ketchup. The general idea is to scoop up the ketchup with the tator tots and get it into your mouth before the ketchup drops off the tator tot.

Another good idea is to just use the tator tots in place of hash browns at breakfast. It works quite well.

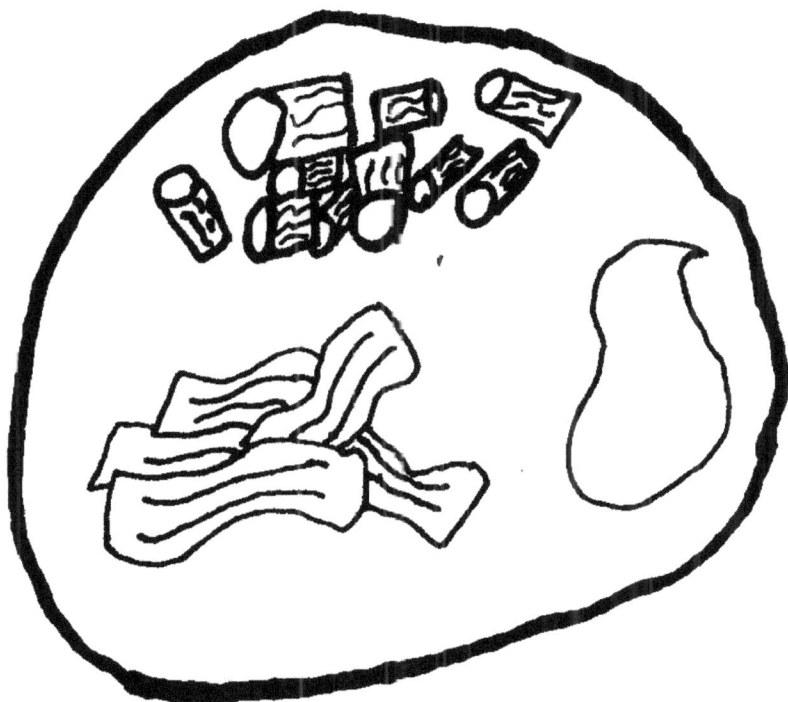

French Toast

French Toast is great. Its simple and different. I really don't know why they call it French Toast. Did it come from France or was it originally made from French bread? Somebody out there send us the answer.

You can serve French Toast with eggs and/or bacon sausage or ham, or fresh fruit such as strawberries, blue berries or apples.

Ingredients

- eggs
- cinnamon
- vanilla extract
- cooking oil
- bread (prefer wheat or French)
- milk
- butter
- nutmeg

Directions

Let the little ones make the batter for the French Toast. Start by cracking open two eggs into a bowl, add 1/4 cup of milk, a teaspoon of vanilla extract, a little cinnamon and nutmeg if you have it. Beat the eggs with the fork until it is all mixed together.

Lightly cover the bottom of the frying pan with cooking oil. When the oil is hot. Dip the bread into the batter real quickly and place it in the frying pan, 3 or 4 pieces at a time. Turn over when lightly browned on each side.

Butter the French Toast after taking from the skillet. Serve with syrup or powdered sugar, meat, eggs, and fresh fruit.

Lunch Recipes

Daddy Dogs

Daddy Dogs are not so different. They are easy to fix and enjoyable to eat. It's hot dogs on toasted cheese bread and add a couple of sliced tomatoes.

Ingredients

- hot dogs (or turkey sausage)
- cheese
- tomatoes
- bread
- mustard and ketchup

Directions

Boil the hot dogs (or turkey sausage) as you normally would. While the hot dogs are boiling warm-up the oven to 350 degrees. Place the bread on the cookie sheet. Place the sliced cheese on the bread. Put bread in oven for not more than a couple of minutes - only long enough for the cheese to melt a little bit. Place the hot dogs and sliced tomatoes on the melted cheese on the bread.

Add mustard, ketchup, pickles, relish, lettuce or whatever is desired.

Serve with fruit punch and chips.

Chili Cheese Dogs

Chili Cheese Dogs is an enhancement over the Daddy Dogs and a little more sloppy too. We add a few twists and make it a more enjoyable and involved meal.

Ingredients

- hot dogs
- cheese
- chili
- hot dog buns
- pickles
- mustard and ketchup

Directions

Boil the hot dogs as you normally would. While the hot dogs are cooking - open the can of chili; empty into the second pot and warm it.

Put a hot dog bun on each plate. Place cheese on the hot dog buns. Place the a cooked hot dog on the hot dog bun. Add sliced cheese and cover with chili. Wow!

The only difference between Chili Cheese Dogs and Daddy Dogs is first the chili and second, we don't toast the buns with this dish, but you could if you wanted to.

Add mustard or ketchup. You can eat with your hands or with a knife and fork.

Serve with fruit punch, sliced pickles, chips and a smile.

Egg Salad and Cheez-Its®

Egg Salad and Cheez-Its is a great lunch treat or snack. Get your fingers right in there.

Ingredients
- 3 eggs
- 1/4 onion
- garlic powder
- 1 tablespoon of mustard
- 2 or 3 tablespoons of mayonnaise
- red pepper

Directions

While the 3 eggs are boiling cut up 1/4 onion into real small chunks. Peel the boiled eggs and cut them into 1/4 inch pieces, Season with garlic powder and pepper to your desired taste. Mix in the mustard and mayonnaise.

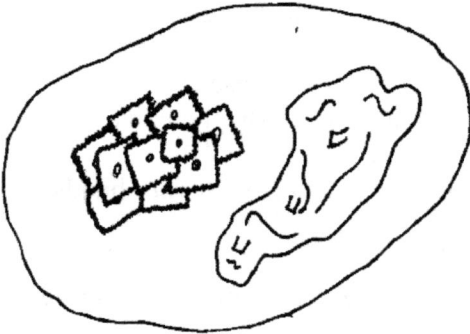

Serve as a dip.

Dip the Cheez-Its (or any cracker or bread of choice) into the egg salad.

Carefully bring the morsel to the tip of our tongue and pull it in quickly. Wow!

Tuna and Crackers

One of my grandmothers made the best tuna in the world - and then she put it on crackers. This is one of the most memorable treats I ever had for lunch. Tuna and Crackers can put a smile on a child that last for the whole afternoon. Coupled with a few card games at the kitchen table and you have another memory in the making.

Ingredients

- 6 once can of tuna
- onion
- bell pepper
- mayonnaise, mustard, relish (optional)
- black pepper, garlic powder
- crackers

Directions

Empty the can of tuna into a mixing bowl. Add one chopped small onion, 1/4 small bell pepper-chopped, 2 or 3 tablespoons of mayonnaise, 1 teaspoon of mustard, 1 teaspoon relish (optional). Season with black pepper and garlic powder. Combine ingredients with a fork.

When mix is completed, spread on crackers, Serve on a plate or platter. Eat as much as you want while playing card games - be careful - the tuna makes the cards stick together.

Wash down with fruit punch.

Hot Dogs, Crackers and Cheese

Hot Dogs, Crackers and Cheese is a small spread for the eaters who like a feast in the round.

Ingredients

- 2 hot dogs per person
- crackers
- cheese
- mustard and mayonnaise

Directions

Slice hot dogs into 1/2 inch slices. Place in frying pan in a 1/4 to 1/2 inch of water. Turn fire under frying pan to medium (keep a close watch on the hot dogs). As the water begins to evaporate - stir hot dogs so they don't stick to the frying pan. Continue to stir the hot dogs until the water is all gone - or pour the water out when the hot dogs are cooked. Once the water is out of the frying pan let the hot dogs brown a little bit. Remove hot dogs from frying pan and place on a plate.

Cut cheese slices into 1 inch squares. Mix 2 tablespoons of mustard with two tablespoons of mayonnaise in a bowl.

Serve hot dogs and cheese on a plate with the crackers. Spread the mustard and mayonnaise mix on each cracker, top with cheese and hot dog, open wide and stuff it in.

Leftover Turkey and Crackers

Left-Over Turkey and Crackers is a great and quick meal. Grab the turkey (or chicken) from the refrigerator, pull the crackers from cabinet. Dump both onto a plate and dig in. No mess, no fix-it-up, no problems and wham-o there it is.

Try a little mustard or mayonnaise, some cheese and a little soda or punch to wash it down.

Ingredients

- left-over turkey (or chicken)
- crackers
- mustard or mayonnaise

Directions

Just do it.

Netfa's Platter

Netfa's Platter is a wish-list of a spread. All the good things my son Netfa likes to see on his plate of cold cuts and then some. Use your own creativity and expand the list of items to fit your child's desire.

Ingredients

- ham
- turkey
- balogna
- salami
- cheese
- green olives
- pickles
- mustard
- crackers

Directions

Slice the above ingredients. Add more for your individual taste. Arrange attractively on a plate or platter. Serve with a movie or table games - or just have it for lunch. Let the young ones decide which items to include and let them arrange the platter to suit their taste.

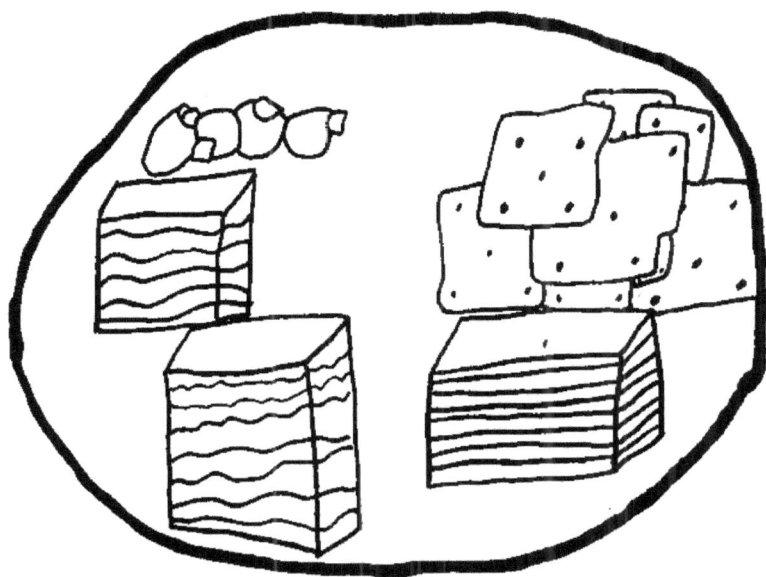

Serve with a special drink. See our Drinks Section to choose one.

Pretzels and Soup

When I was a boy I always wanted to eat my chicken noodle soup with pretzels instead of crackers. And so now as an adult I can do it without getting into trouble! But - with my sons.

Pretzels and Soup is the fulfillment of a life-long dream. And why not, crackers and pretzels are made out of practically the same thing and both have salt on top. Have you ever seen a pretzel floating in a bowl of soup. Just imagine that - then try it. You'll be a Pretzels and Soup convert too.

Pretzels and Soup can also be handy when you might be trying to get a little one to eat soup when they don't want to. Use the pretzels as an incentive.

Ingredients
- soup
- pretzels

Directions

Heat soup. Put in bowl. Let your child place or dip pretzels into soup as desired and eat at will! Soup could be hot – be careful.

VERY IMPORTANT - Please follow the Pretzel Advisory on the next page!

CAUTION: PRETZEL ADVISORY

Avoid the U.F.S. problem. Do not - we repeat - DO NOT put pretzels into the soup too early because they get soggy. And, nobody likes soggy pretzels. The best way to handle this is to put the pretzels in one or two at a time as you are ready to eat them. I'm sure as you try this you will become a Pretzel and Soup expert.

However - if you don't follow this PRETZEL WARNING your pretzels may become what is know as a "U.F.S" - that is - an Unidentified Food Substance.

ENJOY!!

The Hero

One day when we were getting the ingredients for Lumpy Burgers (See Dinner Section) we couldn't find the rolls in the store. So we brought a two foot long French bread roll. Later when Dad was cutting the roll into thirds I (Asiedu) thought we should make a hero out of the giant roll. And below we have it.

Ingredients

- turkey
- pastrami
- balogna
- onions
- mustard
- green olives
- tomatoes

- ham
- salami
- cheese
- pickles
- mayonnaise
- hero bread roll
- lettuce

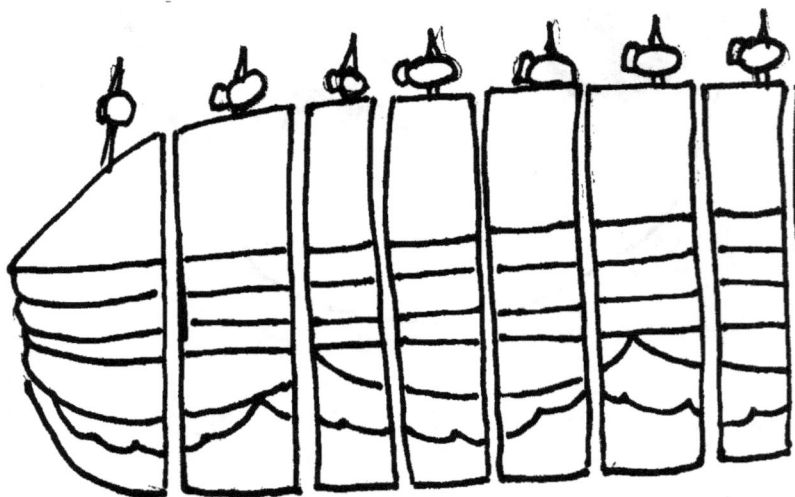

Directions

Slice the tomatoes, onions and pickles very thin and anything else that needs slicing before your start (lettuce, cheese).

Slice the bread roll in half the long way. Put mustard on the top half and mayonnaise on the bottom half. Put one layer of each of the following on the bottom half in this order: ham, pastrami, bologna, salami, turkey, cheese, lettuce, tomatoes, onions, pickles.

Put the top part of the bread on the sandwich. Put toothpicks into the sandwich about one and one-half inches apart (one for each section that will be cut). Put green olives on each of the toothpicks. Slice between the toothpicks.

This sandwich goes good with Monopoly or any other board game.

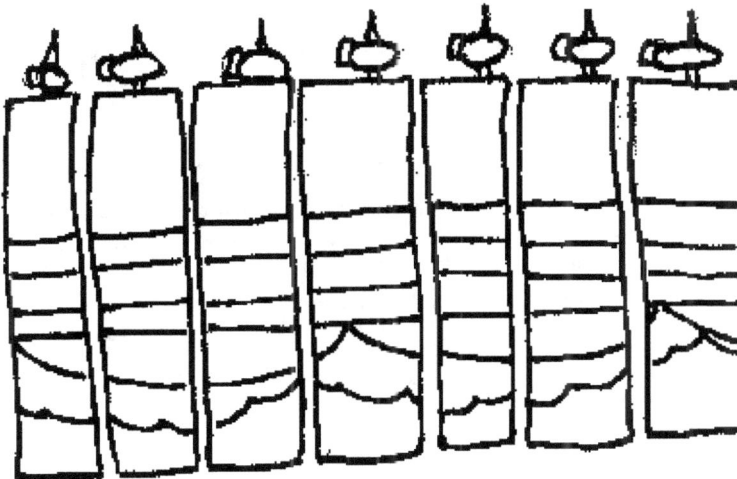

The rest of
the Hero

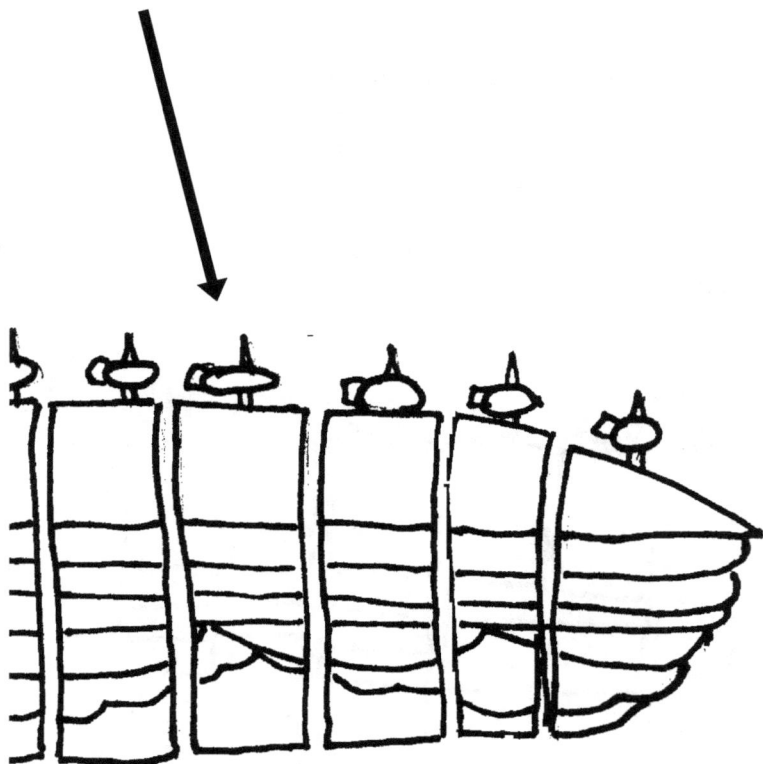

Turkey, Lettuce, Cheese and Potato Chip Sandwich

Now I know this sounds a little strange - BUT...every boy likes to put potato chips on his sandwich at some time or another. That's how the Turkey, Lettuce, Cheese and Potato Chip Sandwich was created. It's what I call the TLC Sandwich. My sons came up with the chips part and I insisted on the lettuce. It wasn't bad. Kind of liked it myself.

Ingredients

- smoked turkey (or leftover turkey)
- bread
- lettuce
- potato ships
- cheese
- mustard and mayonnaise

Directions

First make any "normal" sandwich with the ingredients above or any that you choose. Right before you bite into the sandwich - rip it open and put in a couple of layers of potato chips.

Open wide and listen for the crunch as you bite down.

Ummmmm

The Twist

Twists are exactly that - a twist. The boys created this delicatessen on their own.

Ingredients

- cold cuts (pastrami, turkey, bologna, salami, ham or pastrami)
- cheese
- toppings (mustard and/or mayonnaise)

Directions

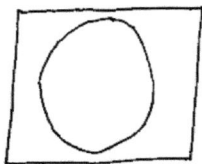

Place 1 slice of cold cuts on 1 slice of cheese or vice-versa.

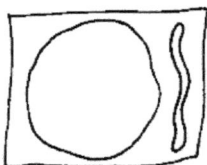

Put your favorite spread (mustard or mayonnaise) at one end.

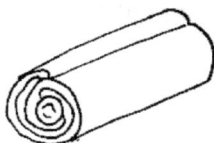

Then roll it up.

Next, eat it.

Crackers or chips on the side is a winner.

Dinner Recipes

Mess 'em Up Jax

Mess 'em Up Jax is a real fun meal. The whole family can participate in planning, making and eating. We call it Mess 'em Up Jax because this is a fun meal that you eat with your fingers by dipping tortilla chips into your favorite meat sauce, piling on some cheese, pickles and other delights - then stuff it into your mouth.

Mess 'em Up Jax can be elaborate or you can make it real simple. However you do it - it's fun to eat.

You can make the meat sauce from scratch following the directions below or just get taco mix or spaghetti mix from the grocery store and mix it in with the ground meat (turkey or beef).

Ingredients (for 4)

- 1 large bag of your favorite tortilla or potato chips
- sliced pickles
- pitted black olives or green olives with pimentos
- cheddar cheese (graded by hand)
- optional: sliced carrots, celery
- *Meat Sauce:* 1½ pounds of ground meat, 1 large onions, 1 large bell pepper, cumin, chili powder, thyme, garlic powder, pepper, 1 8 ounce can of tomato sauce

Directions

While you are browning the ground meat in a large frying pan, add the seasoning: garlic, pepper, chili powder, thyme, cumin, chili powder and chopped onion and bell pepper. Just before the meat is cooked all the way add the tomato sauce.

If you are using the taco or spaghetti mix - add that instead of this list.

Lower the fire, cover and let simmer for 15 minutes. You might need to add a few ounces of water. However, the sauce should not be thin; it should be thick.

Your child can prepare the spread while the meat is cooking. This will be exciting for them while waiting for the big feast. Place the olives, pickles, graded cheese and chips in separate bowls.

Serving

Place the bowls on the table in banquet style. Give each person their own bowl of Mess 'em Up Jax meat sauce and a plate. Let everyone scoop up as much of any of the items they want (into their own bowl or plate). Everything is to be eaten by scooping to the mouth with the chips - no forks or spoons please. DIG IN with your fingers.

For a nutritional supplement I serve with a green salad - which must be eaten first. I've never seen boys eat a salad so fast until I put this spread in front of them and told them they couldn't touch it until the salad was gone.

PS. Have plenty of napkins available.

Fried Chicken Sandwich

This is one of the many fun dishes that was spontaneously created. This meal was discovered one hot spring day in Harlem, New York. We were grabbing some quick fried chicken from a take out joint.

One day when the boys and I were there we noticed the tauter sauce that was on the counter for people who ordered fish sandwiches. What a combination: fried chicken breast, hot sauce and tarter sauce on wheat bread - WOW!

We would normally stand at the counter and eat our chicken covered with tauter sauce, dipping it in hot sauce and watching all the folks who came in to order food.

Now we make this dish ourselves.

Ingredients

- chicken breast
- wheat bread
- tarter sauce
- hot sauce

If you are going to fry your own chicken you'll need, flour, oil, garlic, paprika and pepper.

Directions

Pre-heat the oil on a medium high fire. Season the chicken pieces with garlic, pepper, and paprika (seasoning salt if

you choose). Put three pieces of chicken into a bag with flour in it.
Shake well to coat the chicken with flour.

Put chicken in frying pan. A 12 inch frying pan will take 6-
8 pieces. Cook chicken on one side until brown, turn over to cook
on the other side. Takes about 15-20 minutes on each side. Check
to see that chicken is cooked all the way by slicing open a piece.
(To speed up cooking you can poke holes in the chicken with the
cooking fork or a knife before you coat it with flour.)

Once the chicken breasts are cooked strain them on paper
towels on a plate.

The sandwich is made by placing the chicken on the wheat
bread. I like to put the tarter sauce and hot sauce on the side and
dip my sandwich into it. Its delicious. If you're really
adventurous, skip the bread and use crackers instead.

Asiedu's
Finger Foods

Asiedu's Finger Foods is a feast and a spread. Go to the store. Get all the finger foods you can get. Oh, you might ask, "What are finger foods?" Finger Foods are foods you eat with your fingers. Aren't you glad you asked?

Finger foods are the frozen foods that you can pop into the oven or microwave to warm and then eat with your fingers. Let the children choose the finger foods they like to eat.

Ingredients

- egg rolls
- pizza rolls
- chicken nuggets
- fish sticks
- tator tots
- and whatever else you find in the frozen foods at your grocery store. For vegetables fix something you can eat with your fingers and is very nutritious: trees - I mean broccoli or fresh carrots. Fix a dip to go alone with this meal: mustard, ketchup, bar-b-que sauce or a mixture.

Directions

Pre-heat oven to the average temperature asked for on the individual packages. Spread the foods out on the cookie sheets. Cook/warm until all is ready.

Eat with your fingers. Play a card game or table game during this meal. It's real fun and not messy at all.

Buffalo Wings

Now that Buffalo Wings have become a national tradition, everybody has their own recipe. Here's mine - unique in that it is simple, easy to make and good to eat!

Ingredients

- chicken wings
- butter
- hot sauce
- garlic powder
- paprika
- cooking oil
- soy sauce

Directions

Step One: Prepare the Wings

Season the wings with garlic powder, paprika and a dash of soy sauce. Deep fry in frying pan. Strain all grease off the wings.

Step Two: Prepare the Buffalo

Melt butter with a little hot sauce in a large frying pan on a low fire. Sauté the wings in the butter-hot sauce, then place in a bowl. Do not strain.

Simple, but good. Add more hot sauce to your individual taste. Dip in blue cheese dressing, sour cream or another dip for a real treat.

Lumpy Burgers

Lumpy Burgers are tasty. Besides the good taste - they are easy and quick to make. It will be a great meal for you and your sons.

Ingredients

- ground turkey or beef
- bread rolls
- cheese
- onions
- tomatoes
- lettuce
- garlic powder
- pepper

Directions

Pre-heat the oven to 350 degrees. Have your son put 2 pounds of ground meat in mixing bowl with one large onion that you chopped into ½ inch pieces. Season with garlic powder and pepper. Let him mix with his hands. Make into large hamburger patties (makes about 6). Put patties on frying pan and place in the oven. Let cook. Turn over in about 15 minutes. Make sure the meat is cooked all the way.

Prepare the bread while the patties are cooking. Slice the bread rolls into half (top and bottom). Place open faced on a cookie sheet. Grade the cheese right onto the open bread rolls - as much or as little as you like.

When the patties are almost cooked put the bread into the oven for not more than 3 minutes - just enough for the cheese to begin to melt. Don't leave in too long or the bread will get hard.

Take bread out of the oven. Put patties on the bread and finish with sliced tomatoes, lettuce and pickles if you like. A little mustard and ketchup tops it off well. Open real wide and push it in.

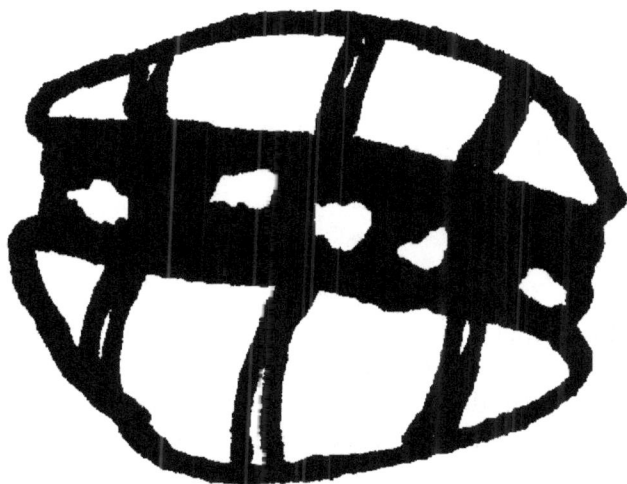

Chicken Wings

Every child enjoys fried Chicken Wings. Fried Chicken Wings can be a dish served by itself or it can be the basis of a larger meal. Fried Chicken Wings is fun to eat and tasty too.

Ingredients

- chicken wings
- flour
- garlic
- pepper
- paprika
- cooking oil
- soy sauce

Directions

If the chicken wings are whole, cut them at the joint into three pieces. Use only the larger two pieces.

Let the children season the wings with garlic, pepper, paprika and a dash of soy sauce. Place 10 to 15 wings at a time in the bag of flour. Shake to cover the wings with flour.

Pre-heat about one-half inch of cooking oil in skillet to a medium-high fire. Let the adult drop the wings (one at a time) into the frying pan. Put only enough wings in the frying pan that are covered by the cooking oil. Cook the wings until they are golden brown. It should take less than 20 minutes - but test by slicing open a wing to make sure it is cooked all the way.

When wings are cooked - place chicken on paper towels to strain the grease. Make sure you cook a lot because this is one of the best meals going.

Uncle Siasa's Grilled Chicken Sandwich
- With Pickles -

Uncle Siasa's Grilled Chicken Sandwich - With Pickles came from an improvised meal at my good friend's house one Saturday evening. We went to the freezer and found some frozen chicken steaks. Popped them into the oven and began to create. What a discovery!

Ingredients

- frozen chicken steaks, breasts or cultets
- hamburger buns
- lettuce
- tomatoes
- mustard, ketchup and mayonnaise
- cheese optional
- and most importantly: PICKLES

Directions

Cook the frozen chicken according to the directions on the box. After the chicken is cooked let the children create their own sandwiches with the ingredients supplied - only one rule - Uncle Siasa insist that everyone must have pickles, I mean lots of pickles, all over their entire sandwich. Have fun.

Serve with ruffled potato chips and a salad.

Homemade Pizza

Homemade Pizza is relatively simple to make and can be a great activity and cooking lesson for both dads and sons. One of the greatest rewards from this activity is the sense of satisfaction and pride from having put together this creation and say "we did it!"

Ingredients

- pizza dough comes in a can like biscuits (rectangle shape) or already prepared (round)
- tomato sauce
- cheese
- olives
- pepperoni
- mushrooms
- whatever other topping you like
- Seasoning: garlic powder, pepper, chili powder, paprika, thyme, Italian seasoning, oregano

Directions

Pre-heat the oven according to directions on pizza dough package. Spread a very thin layer of butter on the cookie sheet. Lay out the pizza dough on the cookie sheet. (Follow the directions on the package. Note: Some packages want you to cook the dough for a few minutes before placing the ingredients on the pizza dough.)

To make the pizza sauce, put the tomato sauce and small amounts of the seasoning in a bowl (garlic powder, Italian seasoning, paprika, thyme, chili powder and oregano) or buy it in the bottle from the grocery store.

Let the children do the assembling of the pizza - with your help Let the children do the assembly of the pizza with you help and supervision.

Spread pizza sauce very thinly over the pizza dough. Sprinkle the graded cheese all over the pizza sauce on the pizza dough. Sprinkle the rest of the ingredients - one at a time - all over the cheese.

Cook the pizza 10-15 minutes. (Follow the directions on the package).

After pizza is cooked, let it sit for a few minutes then cut and serve.

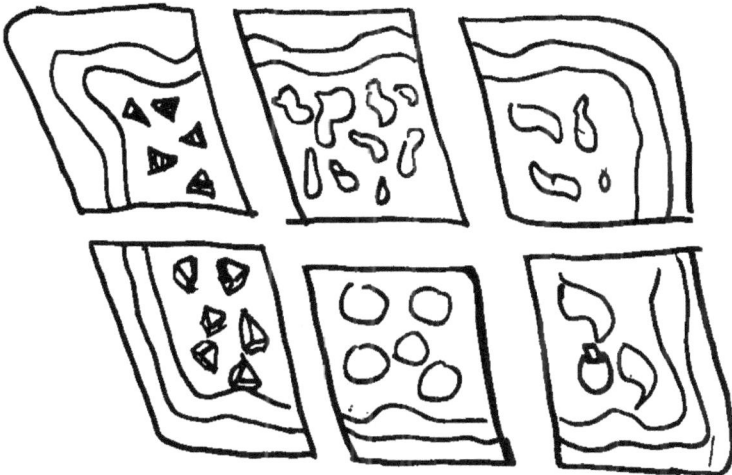

Watch for the smiles on the little one's faces as they realize they made their own pizza.

Pizza Dogs

Pizza Dogs are fantastic and delicious. I love Pizza Dogs. You and your crew will find this a great treat that you will want to come back to again and again.

Ingredients

- pizza
- hot dogs

Directions

You can make pizza using the Homemade Pizza recipe on the previous page or just get pizza from a pizza shop or cook frozen pizza from the grocery store. Decide which pizza you will use.

Boil the hot dogs. After the hot dogs are cooked, roll the hot dogs in the pizza slices and stick a tooth pick through the pizza dog to keep it from unrolling.

You can add mustard if you like or just bite into them as is. On a Saturday night this makes a great meal with a simple green salad and a video from your local video rental store.

Mexican Tacos

Mexican Tacos is a great way to get the children involved. Make a list together of the ingredients to buy, then shop and prepare the meal together. The great reward is the huge smile on the child's face as they take that first big bite from a delicious Mexican Taco.

Ingredients

Keep it simple - get the Taco mix from the store - plus:
- 2 pounds of ground meat (turkey or beef)
- 1 onion
- 1/2 small bell pepper
- cheddar cheese
- Taco Sauce
- olives
- taco shells
- tomatoes
- lettuce

Directions

To cook the ground meat follow the instructions on the Taco mix package that you got from the store. (Optional: While the meat is browning, add the chopped onion and bell pepper.

While the meat sauce is cooking you can help your son grade the cheese (be careful), wash and chop the tomatoes into small pieces and slice the lettuce into small pieces. Put the cheese, tomatoes, lettuce, pickles etc. into separate bowls. Arrange all the bowls on the table for self-service.

When the meat is cooked and all the toppings are ready - slightly warm the taco shells on cooking sheet in the oven at 350 degrees for not more than 5 minutes. Let everyone prepare their own tacos. Put the meat in first, cheese next and then go for it.

Don't skimp on the vegetables.

Outdoor Dishes

Grilled Hamburgers

Grilled Hamburgers is one of the simplest and most rewarding outdoor dishes. It can also be done indoors in the oven or broiler. (See Lumpy Burgers in the Dinner section.) Children can make the hamburger paddies. They love it because it gives them a chance to get their hands in everything.

Ingredients

- ground turkey, chicken or beef
- onions
- garlic powder
- red pepper

Directions

Take two pounds of hamburger meat, chop one large onion into small pieces. Place both in large bowl, season with garlic and pepper, mix with your clean hands until it is thoroughly mixed.

Shape meat with your hands into the desired number of paddies (5-7). Cook on grill until done. Remember to check the inside to make sure meat is cooked all the way. You can add bar-b-que sauce if desired when the meat is about two-thirds of the way cooked.

Serve on hamburger buns with ketchup, pickles, lettuce, tomatoes and cheese.

Yellow Chicken

Yellow Chicken is what happens when you season your chicken with a little turmeric. It turns yellow.

Ingredients

- chicken
- turmeric
- red pepper
- soy sauce (or Bragg®)
- garlic

Directions

First, while the grill outside is getting hot prepare the chicken.

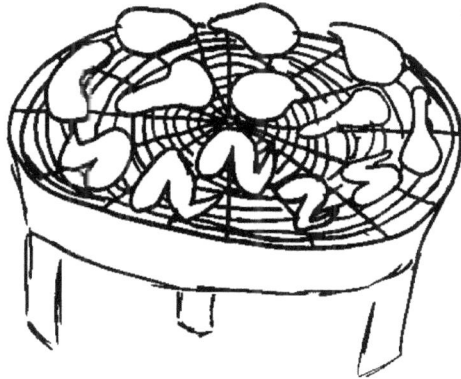

Take the skin off the chicken (I like to just use thighs but you can use any or all chicken parts), wash chicken pieces and place in a large bowl. Season with turmeric, red pepper, soy sauce, and garlic. Cook on the grill until done - turning periodically. You will note that after the chicken is cooked it will be a yellowish color - and tasty.

Serve with a green salad and bread.

Roasted Marshmallows

Roasted Marshmallows is the first thing on our list when we go camping. If I don't bring the marshmallows then I have to stay home because my sons won't allow me on the trip. Roasted Marshmallows are easy to do and fun to eat.

Ingredients

- marshmallows

Directions

Build a safe camp fire. Un-tie the hook on the metal clothes hangers. Straighten the hangers out so children won't have to get to close to the fire.

Let the children put the marshmallows on the end of the hangers - not more than two at a time. Put the hangers with the marshmallows directly into the fire or just above the flames. Let the marshmallows heat up until they turn brown. This takes only a few seconds, sometimes longer. Blow on them to cool. Eat with gusto. (Caution: don't let children touch the end of the hanger when it comes out of the fire for the metal will be HOT!)

This is a great activity beginning with building the camp fire to stuffing your face with the delicious roasted marshmallows. Not only are you making Roasted Marshmallows here - you are also making something for your children that will last a lot longer - for even an eternity: its called fond memories.

Hanger Hot Dogs

Hanger Hot Dogs is the greatest lunch in the forest. This meal works great on camping trips or in your backyard.

Ingredients

- hot dogs
- hot dog buns
- mustard and ketchup

Directions

Build a safe camp fire. Let everyone put their own hot dogs on their hanger the long way. Hold the hot dogs over the fire just above the flame until cooked. Don't put them too close to flame because they will cook on the outside and not on the inside. Give it time (5-10 minutes each) Put hot dogs in buns, add mustard and/or ketchup.

Serve with potato chips and drinks. Great time!

Be careful of the <u>hot</u> hangers.

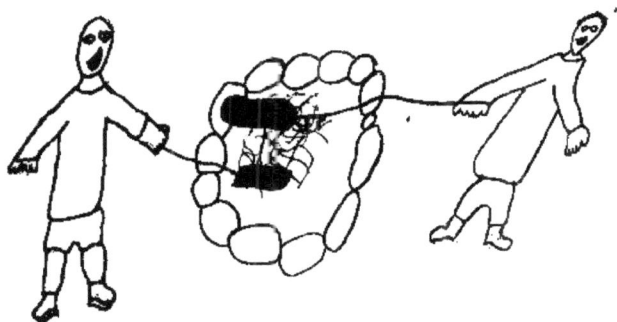

Take some pictures!

Drinks

AGC Fizz

AGC Fizz was created by Netfa at a bar-b-que at my friends' house, Phyllis and Paul. On one of his many trips to the cooler for something to drink he mixed apple juice, ginger ale and cola. Boys like to mix their drinks so it doesn't surprise me that he came up with this. It wasn't too bad either.

Ingredients

- apple juice
- ginger ale
- cola

Directions

Mix equal parts (or to taste) of apple juice, ginger ale and cola.

Drink - It tastes deliciously delicious.

OJ and 7-Up®

OJ and 7-Up is a special drink that my boys love. Its special because its different. Children, especially boys, like to mix flavors.

Ingredients

- orange juice
- 7-Up (or any colorless drink like ginger ale or Sprite®)

Directions

Make each of these drinks individually. You don't want a pitcher full to go flat. Plus, each time you drink it - you might want a different percentage of each. One time you might want it to be stronger in OJ and the next time stronger with 7-Up.

You can do this best in either of two ways. First, its good just to give it to the boys without telling them ahead of time. It will make them feel special because you gave them something special.

Second, you can tell them you have the ingredients in the refrigerator and they can help themselves when they are ready. This works great on a hot boring day. Live a little. Be creative. It works.

HomeMade Lemonade

Lemonade is so easy to make even you or I can do it. But having the kids do it is even more fun. Be careful they might want to go into business.

Once you teach the children to make this drink they'll want to do it over and over again. Take them to the store to get the lemons first - always get extra lemons - you might need them.

Ingredients

- 4 lemons
- water
- sugar

Directions

Before you cut open the lemons squeeze them and rub and role them on the counter to soften them up. Wash the lemons thoroughly. Cut each lemon in half and squeeze out all the juice and pulp into the pitcher. Cut each lemon into quarters and put into pitcher.

In a separate container add one-half cup of sugar with one cup of warm or hot water. (You do this because sugar mixes with hot water better than it mixes with cold water.) Add the sugared water to the pitcher. Add 3 quarts of water and 1 tray of ice to the pitcher. Stir thoroughly. Taste it. Feel free to add more lemon or sugar to suit your taste.

Remember to mix the sugar with warm or hot water otherwise the sugar will not mix properly and will just sink to the bottom of the container and you won't taste it.

Next: pour large glasses of lemonade and sip this refreshing liquid while you relax and enjoy your day. Find a place to put your feet up (try under a shady tree) - all of you - while you sip.

Don't forget to say "AHHHHHHH!" after your first sip.

Fruit Punch and Lemonade

This is a nice little diversion and an inexpensive treat for the kids. Fruit Punch and Lemonade is also easy to make.

Ingredients

- fruit punch
- lemonade

Directions

Mix equal parts of fruit punch (or any punch) with lemonade. You can get frozen, bottled or powder mix for the fruit punch or the lemonade and mix them.

Also available in this section of Fun Meals is a recipe for lemonade which is excellent if I must say so myself. Its easy to do, fun to make and inspiring upon completion

Grape Juice and Orange Juice

Grape Juice and Orange Juice is the most exciting and refreshing drink on earth that kids can make on their own. They love it. It becomes their creation. They feel like they're making something.

Ingredients

- grape juice
- orange juice

Directions

Put equal parts of grape juice and orange juice into a large pitcher. Stir and drink until your heart's content.

Serve outside if possible with cookies or chips on the side.

What a cool treat!.

Chocolate Explosion

Chocolate Explosion is a simple drink with variations on a theme. In its simplest form its seltzer and chocolate milk. In its most developed form it's and an explosion of a dessert.

Ingredients

- seltzer water
- chocolate milk
- options: ice cream, whipped cream, cherries, chocolate candy

Directions

For the simple version: mix equal parts (or to taste) seltzer and chocolate milk.

For the advanced and exciting version: put a scoop of vanilla or chocolate ice cream in the glass first, add equal parts of chocolate milk and seltzer water. Add whipped cream on top and throw in a cherry and some chopped chocolate on top for good measure. Man, what a pick-me-up for a child who's in need of a little excitement.

Breads

Garlic and Cheese Bread

Cheese and Garlic Bread is always a winner. I learned this from my mother 20-30 years ago and it always goes over with a bang.

Ingredients

- French or Italian bread loaf
- cheese (cheddar & Monterey jack)
- butter
- garlic powder
- dried parsley
- paprika

Directions

Slice the bread in half the long way so that you separate the top from the bottom. Butter both halves of the bread lightly. Cut the bread into two-inch slices - keeping the bread together. (In actuality you want to slice through the bread about ninety-five percent through so the bread stays together.)

Place each half of the bread on a piece of foil. Sprinkle the garlic powder lightly over the bread. Grade the two kinds of cheese over the bread lightly, Sprinkle the parsley and paprika over the bread. Close the foil almost all the way. Do not press down on the foil - or the cheese will stick to it. Put wrapped bread on the cookie sheet.

Place in oven at 350 degrees for 10 minutes or until the cheese melts. This bread is delicious! Goes great with spaghetti.

Cheese Toast

Cheese Toast is so simple to make and there are many ways to enhance it with your own creativity.

Ingredients

- bread
- cheese

Directions

Pre-heat oven to broil. Place cheese on slices of bread. Put bread on cookie sheet in the broiler of the oven for only a quick two minutes. Remove. Cheese should be melted and ready for eating.

You can place anything on top of the cheese such as lunch meat or bacon.

See Daddy Dogs (Lunch) and Bacon on Cheese Bread (Bread) for suggestions.

This Cheese Toast also goes good for - or with - any breakfast or dinner.

Bacon on Cheese Bread

Bacon on Cheese Bread is an enhancement over Cheese Toast. It is also simple to make.

Ingredients

- bacon
- bread
- cheese

Directions

Cook the desired amount of bacon (suggest 2 pieces per piece of bread).

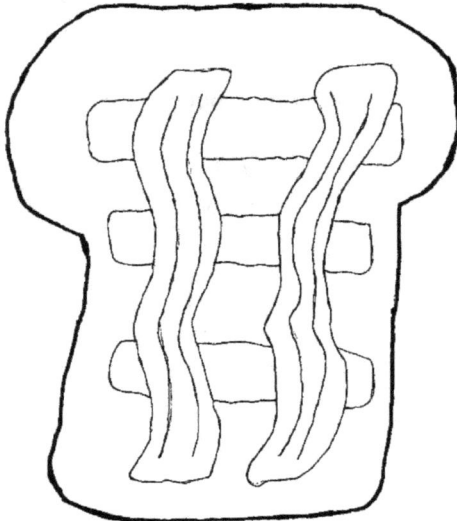

Pre-heat oven to broil. Place cheese on slices of bread. Place 2 strips of cooked bacon crossways on top of the cheese.

Put bread on cookie sheet in the broiler of the oven for only a quick minute.

Remove, let cool and eat.

Quite a treat!

Potatoes

Tator Tots®

Tator Tots can go with any meal, breakfast, lunch, dinner or by themselves. They are easy to make and sold in almost every food store.

Ingredients

- 12-15 tator tots each
- garlic powder
- pepper
- paprika

Directions

Pre-heat oven according to the directions on the tator tots package. After spreading the tator tots on a cookie sheet - season lightly with garlic powder, pepper, and paprika.

Cook in the oven according to the directions (usually around ten minutes). When cooked and ready to eat you can dip the Tator Tots into ketchup, mustard or a mixture of both.

See Bacon, Tator Tots and Ketchup in the Breakfast sction of this book

Silver Dollar French Fries

Silver Dollar French Fries will excite any youth - or adult for that matter. This is one of my special creations that goes good by itself or with hamburgers or fish.

Ingredients

- potatoes
- powdered garlic
- paprika
- pepper
- cooking oil

Directions

Clean several large potatoes. Do not peel them. Cut the potatoes into thin slices like silver dollars. Heat oil 1/2 inch in bottom of frying pan (medium-high fire). Place potatoes into hot oil - be careful - this is not for children to do! Turn potatoes over once they start to turn brown. Remove from frying pan when done. Strain potatoes on paper towels. Lightly season immediately with garlic powder, paprika and pepper.

This is one tasty treat that's great. It can make any meal just that much more exciting. You can also serve these Silver Dollar French Fries with a dip of your choice or just ketchup.

Boiled Potato Creations

Boiled Potato Creations are very much like baked potatoes - but they are not the same. It's so much easier and quicker.

Ingredients

- potatoes
- toppings: butter, cheese, sour cream, bacon bits, chives, garlic powder, pepper etc.

Directions:

Clean potatoes before you start. Do not peel the potatoes. Cut the potatoes into one-inch cubes. Boil in water for 30 minutes - or until soft. Strain the water off and serve.

Pile the potatoes on the plate and fix 'em up!

I like to smash the potato cubes with a fork before I put the butter on them. A little garlic powder, some red pepper and some bacon bits. You can put anything on the potatoes: sour cream, cheese, chili - you name it. Try it.

Salads

Fruit Salad

Children love Fruit Salad especially if they get to help make it themselves. Fruit Salad is not only good for you - it is good to you. Children love it's fresh and sweet taste.

Ingredients:

- 2 sweet red or green apples
- 3 sweet and delicious pears
- 1/4 large ripe pineapple
- 1/2 pound grapes
- 2 ripe bananas
- 1 ripe kiwi (optional)

Directions

Wash all of the fruit before beginning. Peel the 2 apples and the 2 pears. Cut the core out and slice into 1/3 inch chunks. Peel the 1/4 ripe pineapple, cut into chunks. Pick the grapes of the stems. Peel the 2 bananas and cut into 1/4 inch slices. Peel the Kiwi and cut into 1/8 inch slices. Put all the sliced fruit into a large bowl; toss gently. Store in refrigerator for one hour.

Can be served by itself or with whipped cream.

Busy Salad

I love a Busy Salad and I have no problems getting my sons to eat salad as long as I make it attractive to them. They get to help make the salad and choose their own salad dressing.

Ingredients

Salad for four:
- red leaf lettuce or Romaine lettuce
- carrots
- tomatoes
- mushrooms
- olives
- cucumbers
- pickles are optional

Directions

Wash all the vegetables first. Cut or break 6 large leafs of lettuce into small pieces, slice 4 inches of a carrot into thin slices (use a cheese grader if available), just enough to cover the lettuce. Slice a medium tomato. Slice 4 inches of a cucumber. Add three mushrooms - sliced thin. Add a handful of green or black olives. Let the child mix the salad and serve.

Desserts and Snacks

Kid Pops

Kid Pops is like a home-made icy. It is a great summer cooler-off-er and it also helps to teach responsibility and patience with a little science thrown in. My sons taught me this one.

Ingredients

- fruit punch or fruit drink

Directions

The simplest form of Kid Pops is to pour fruit drink into an ice tray, freeze it and then let the children have them - outside - I might add. But let's take it a little further. My sons like to fill up anything they can get their hands on with fruit drinks - to excess I might add. Here's what I suggest - start with a plan.

Sit down with the kids, explain the idea, write up a plan for what drink and what containers to use. Let the children do all the work. After they have gone to the store with you to purchase the drink, fill the ice trays or other containers. Carefully put them in the freezer. Have the children clean up afterwards; that's where the responsibility comes in. When they have to wait for the liquid to freeze; that's where the patience comes in. How long does it take to freeze?

If you do this in the middle of the day it will seem like an eternity to a young and eager child. But if you prepare the concoction the night before right before the children go to bed, it will be ready when they rise - and they'll also go to bed with a smile on their face and warm feelings in their heart.

Caution: let them eat the Kid Pops outside so no one has to clean up the mess. These things will melt fast on a real hot day.

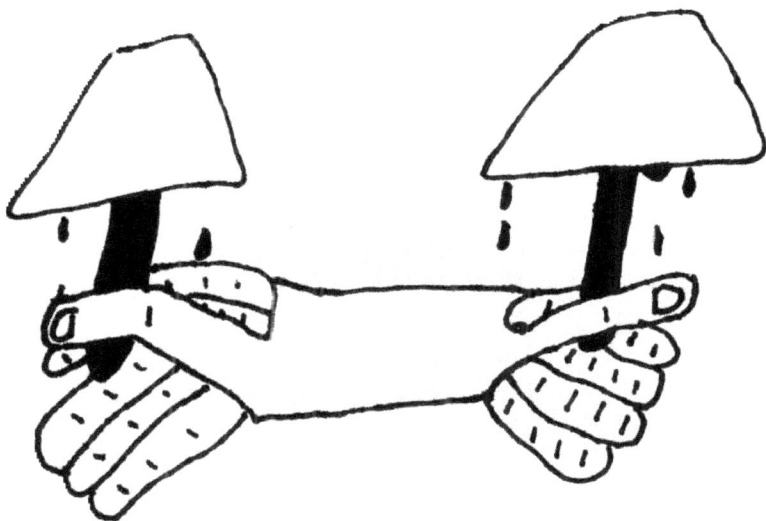

Popcorn and Orange Juice

Popcorn and Orange Juice - my favorite snack - without question. Some people have thought me a little strange - including my two sons - until they tried it.

Ingredients

- popcorn
- orange juice

Directions

Pop the popcorn according to the directions on the container or purchase popcorn already popped. I like to pop mine the old fashion way – in a pot with a little oil and shake it.

Make the orange juice according to the directions on the container or purchase the orange juice already made.

Put the popcorn in big bowl. Pour orange juice into a tall glass.

To eat: take a hand full of popcorn into your mouth and then take a very small sip of orange juice. Now chew and swallow. This is good! Go ahead try it. Admit it - it's great isn't it?

This is a great snack while playing a table game or watching a movie.

Cookies and Ice Cream

One of the greatest desserts in the world for a child is Cookies and Ice Cream. Make the dessert something extra special with your child with a few little enhancements.

Ingredients

- ice cream
- cookies
- whipped cream
- love

Directions

Let the little one serve up the ice cream into the bowls. Next, get the whipped cream out. Let the little one administer the whipped cream onto the mountains of ice cream and then place the cookies decoratively in the whipped cream as they see fit.

The main idea here is to let the children be creative - with your support and admiration. Throw in a little hug as you congratulate them on their artistic abilities.

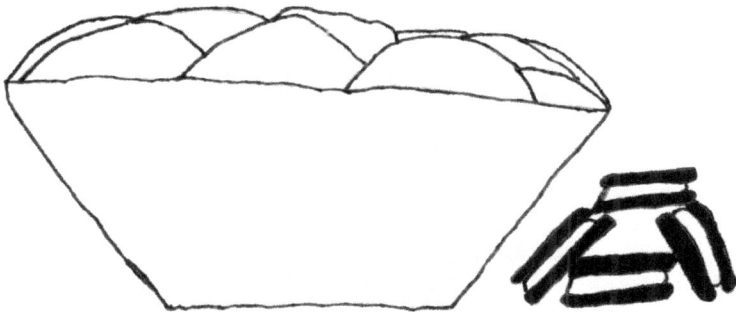

Rootbeer Float

A Rootbeer Float is one my old time favorites. These are fun and easy to make and quite tasty.

Ingredients

- ice cream
- any drink or soda of choice -
  I happen to like vanilla ice cream and rootbeer but you can use any favor ice cream and drink combination. Sometimes I come home with ice cream sandwiches and fruit punch - they love it.

Directions

This is a fun treat that the children can make on their own with a little supervision. Put two large scoops of ice cream into a large glass, add soda or drink up to 1/2 inch from the top of the glass, add whipped cream on top of the ice cream.

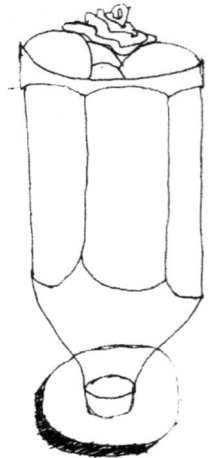

You can also add sprinkles or cherries if you desire. Make sure they clean up after themselves or you'll have melted ice cream running down the side of the counter or table.

Enjoy.

Strawberry Shortcake

The one and only great traditional dessert: Strawberry Shortcake. When I was a child, this was the all-time #1 dessert. This dessert in not only fun to eat, its fun to make.

Ingredients

- strawberries
- shortcake (or pound cake)
- whipped cream

Directions

You can get fresh or frozen strawberries. This recipe calls for fresh strawberries. Everything can be done by the children with minor supervision - or better yet - do it with them.

Wash the strawberries lightly before you start. Cut the stem off the strawberries. Slice them into halves or quarter. Wash them lightly again. Put a slice of cake in the bowl. Cover the cake with strawberries. Cover the strawberries with mountains of whipped cream. Dig in.

This recipe can be used with any kind of fruit or berries for those that choose not to use strawberries. Some of my favorite substitutes are blueberries, peaches, apples, grapes, kiwi or a combination.

Brownies and Whipped Cream

Everything doesn't have to be complicated. Sometimes the simplest things can bring the greatest joy. Brownies and Whipped Cream is a simple joy. You can make brownies from the box, a homemade recipe or buy them already made if you like. This recipe calls for brownies purchased from the bakery (or the grocery store).

Ingredients

- brownies
- whipped cream

Directions

Cut the brownies and place on a saucer. Put tons of whipped cream on the brownies. Eat with your fingers. The real trick is to get the brownies into our mouth without getting whipped cream on your nose.

Have a good time!

Fun Meal Activities

Row, Row, Row Your Boat

One of the greatest joys I've every had was eating lunch in a row boat. Personally I prefer canoes to row boats. But I'll take either. Which one do you think your son will prefer? Whatever the answer - try it. Try both, - and compare.

Pack a couple of special sandwiches and some other treats. Take a short trip to the local park or into the country to rent a boat and you and your child get in. Go to the middle of the lake or just go to another spot, park the boat, eat lunch, take a walk and come back. What a thrill! What an adventure! What a dad!

And don't forget there are also paddle boats - which are a lot more stable. If you don't want to be in a self-powered boat see Boat Ride in this section.

Make sure you obey the safety rules!

Picnic at Work

For a child to get to go to daddy's work is always special. This is a great event for the youth. There are variations on the theme depending on the job situation. The important thing is to have the child meet the father at work, have lunch (or dinner) together and then the father can go back to work. The child gets to spend time with dad and is thus on cloud nine.

Scenario One: The father works long hours in an office. The mother or other helpful person packs a picnic lunch and the kids, travels to the work office at an appointed time. Once arriving at the office and having joyful greetings, the picnic blanket is spread on the floor in the office and the feast follows. After the leisure lunch a little game if time permits and then all parties resume their day's activities. This works great for dads that have to work on Saturdays, Sundays or holidays.

Scenario Two: When you can't have the picnic in the "office" or anywhere in the building where daddy works - take the picnic outside to the front or back lawn of the building or to the neighborhood park. Another option is to buy lunch from the employee's cafeteria. Try to be creative in the location you choose. Remember we're making memories here and creating good feelings for both the parent and the child.

Look through the Lunch Section to see what meals the child can make for daddy.

Deck Sandwich

Not everyone can have a Deck Sandwich simply because you need a deck to have a Deck Sandwich.

Fix a few sandwiches and go sit on the deck and eat them. Nothing fancy. Use your better judgment about taking children out onto the deck and especially leaving them alone or unattended. I recommend this meal time activity only for low decks, not high rises and only for older more responsible children.

Back Yard Dinner

A Back Yard Dinner is usually simple and fun. The food can be prepared in the house and eaten outside. It can be cooked outside and eaten inside. It can even be cooked outside and eaten outside. Just the idea and function of adding the outdoors as part of the meal activity adds a little excitement for a youngster. Get them involved carrying this or that back and forth. Do it together. Teach as you go. Explain. Make them a part of it. Be a team.

Ideal meals for this are Lumpy Burgers, Buffalo Wings or Netfa's Platter.

Midnight Snack

Does your child ever wake up or wind up being up late at night. Well, while the house is all dark and there's no one up except you and the boy(s) - have a snack in the kitchen and talk a little. It's a perfect opportunity to tell your son about some of your childhood memories - some interesting or funny story that will amuse him. Children like to know about their parents when they were kids. It helps them to feel more a part of your life and they feel special to learn about you before you became "big."

Rubber Target

For us, Rubber Target is very special. We get all the little plastic soldiers and action figures and line them up on a dresser top, counter or book case. Each of us gets ten rubber bands and takes turns shooting the rubber men down. We keep score and have a great time. Of course we have to have a big bowl of popcorn or another snack (see Popcorn and OJ in the Snack Section of this book).

Fast Food

Every child likes fast food restaurants! You know the ones - they're everywhere these days. There have been comments about the nutritional value of such food - this is not our subject here. Bonding is our subject. There's no harm in eating fast food from time to time - as long as we don't try to live off of it. Your son will greatly enjoy a quick trip to the local fast food joint to sit and eat with dad. Take him; have a good time, enjoy. Spend a little time talking about what's on his mind, the things that interest him.

Slow Food

A little slow food never hurt anybody either. Slow Food is pretty much the same as Fast Food except you go to a different kind of restaurant. With Slow Food you go to a cafe, or to a neighborhood diner or wherever you can get lunch for you and your son to sit down, talk and eat a meal.

This can be done for breakfast, lunch or dinner or even just a snack or ice cream. The purpose here is for you and the boy to get some time alone dealing with or discussing things of interest to him. Don't make this a time to correct or discipline; make it a time of joy, peace and encouragement.

PanCakes

Pan Cakes are great. You don't have to actually have pancakes. The point of this meal-activity is to go to breakfast together at some restaurant. Just go. Take the kids to have breakfast on a Sunday after or before church or on a Saturday. Have a feast. Enjoy. Spend some time together enjoying the morning hours.

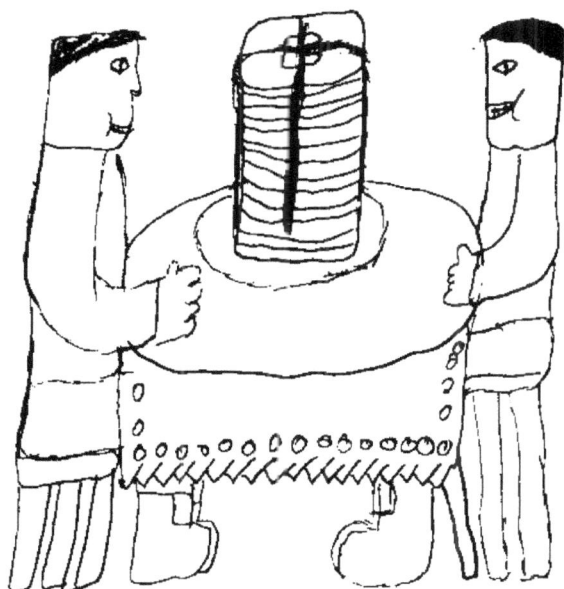

I Scream, You Scream

About one-half hour before bedtime is a good time to take your son out for ice cream. Why then? Because every child likes pleasant and unexpected surprises. Of course this is good when they have earned a special treat with a good report card, an excellent grade on a test or an exam or just for being a good child. Show some love and have a fun time. He will scream for Joy!

Pizza, Pizza

Take the boys - go get a pizza. Eat like a pig, talk, smile and come back home and talk about how good it was for just you and your children to go get a pizza and have some time to yourself. Let it be known how much you enjoy going to get pizza with them. Tell them they're special and that's why you take them to get pizza.

Do this on a regular basis and let the child select which pizza parlor to go to. Eat what they like! Let them order whatever they want no matter how much you might disagree - as long as it's not a danger. Let them exercise their decision-making muscles.

Bike Ride

To take a Bike Ride is easy. Just pack a lunch and set a course to ride to the park. Or just go somewhere on the bike and eat. Use the bikes as an alternate source of transportation instead of the car, bus or truck. (Don't go too far - you want to get back under your own power!)

Doing things differently adds a little spice to life especially for the child who gets to do the same thing in the same way as daddy. For younger children you can get seats mounted on your bike and take them for a ride.

Tour Boat Lunch

Take a tour on a boat. Pack a lunch or buy it on the boat. If weather permits and the boat has the facilities you should sit outside. It's really special that way. It really doesn't matter if the tour goes somewhere you are familiar with or not. What matters is the special activity of being on a boat.

A lot of cities may not have access to a tour boat, cruise ship or even a commuter ferry because of a lack of oceans, rivers or lakes. Take what you can get. If boats are not available to you take a bus outing or a train trip (See Sky King and Have Lunch, Will Travel in the Activities Section). These are all variations on a theme.

Have Lunch, Will Travel

Let's go for a ride - on a train, on a bus, in a car, however you want to travel. Let's just get out and go somewhere - no place special but let's just travel. Pack a lunch, get on a bus or train and ride to the nearest town or to a place you've been wanting to go to.

Eat lunch while you are traveling or once you get there. Do what you have to do or want to do and go back. Make an outing out of it. Make it interesting for the child while you run an errand somewhere - add lunch in a creative atmosphere if possible. Just a little something to remember.

Park It Here

Park it Here puts you, the children, lunch, and a little activity in the neighborhood park.

Keep it simple. Pack a lunch or buy a lunch, go to the park, eat on the grass or picnic table and follow it up with a little football, baseball, basketball, tennis, a walk, or swings and jungle gym. Don't over complicate it. Keep it simple. You're going to the park; you are going to play and you are going to eat lunch. That's it. It's not very time consuming and its relaxing. It's also concentrated quality time with just dad. Its special.

A suggestion: When it is time for lunch ask your son what he would like for lunch, tell him what you would like for lunch. Grab a football on the way out the door, go to the local deli, get a couple of sandwiches, go to park and see what happens.

Mountain High

Mountain High is a drive up to some place where there is a good view of the city or the sky-line. Take a meal or snack and have a seat with just you and your son. Spend the time eating and examining the sights. Get the youngster used to looking at the city from a different perspective. This is something good to do during the day as well as at night. At night you get to see all the pretty lights outlining the city. Water views are excellent too.

A different view will expand his horizon.

Take a Hike

One of the best surprises I gave my sons was when we took a long hike up in the mountains and when we got to top we were all exhausted and hungry. We sat around for a while, drank some water from our bottles, rested and were ready to leave.

Instead of leaving I pulled out a feast from my back pack which caught them completely by surprise. It was Netfa's Platter (See the Lunch Section), complete with crackers, turkey breast, turkey ham, cheese, mustard, mayonnaise, cookies and paper plates.

Boy what a treat and the timing was excellent. Instead of having to make that long hike back on an empty stomach we had a wonderful feast and they were quite motivated.

Tent City

Pitch a tent. Fix lunch. Go inside tent. Eat Lunch. We have this great five person tent. Periodically we will pitch the tent in the back yard or in the neighborhood park. We'll pack a lunch like we're going on a picnic and have a feast right in our own neighborhood.

Sure cuts down on traveling expenses. But then on the other hand we could travel a few miles to a park and pitch the tent there and have lunch. One of the beauties of this is that the boys get practice setting up the tent so that when you do go camping for real they will be ready.

One time we even set-up the tent in the bedroom.

Fish Sandwich

Go fishing. When you go fishing you will need to eat. There you have it. Pack a lunch to eat while you are fishing. An extra special treat would be to catch some fish, clean and cook it all in one day.

Maybe for dinner you could clean it and cook it after you return from fishing - no matter how big or small your catch. This is a great activity while you are camping out. It will be one of the greatest fish stories you've ever told.

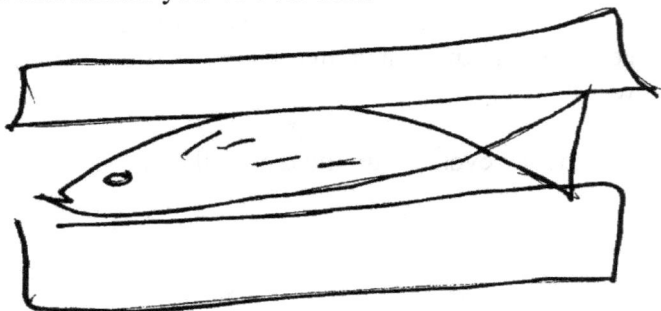

At The Mall

Most of the indoor shopping malls across the country have several eateries for their customers. Take your son to eat his favorite meal in the mall. Just you and him. This can be done while mom is shopping or just the two of you take off on your own to go and eat. Try combining this meal with a trip to the mall for the two of you to pick up something he needs. Take the time and give him a treat.

No Talking
in the Library

The Library is an excellent place to take your child. Go, get some books, read, enjoy the afternoon. Pick up some books for a school project or just for recreational reading, science projects or whatever.

After the library go get something to eat. Talk about the books you picked up; read to each other. Live a little.

Sky King

What is Sky King. Sky King is the king of the sky. And if there is any way you can take your son on a joy ride in a small plane - do it - he will feel like he is king of the sky. Where do you find such planes? Keep in mind that a helicopter flight could be just as rewarding. Where I live there are pilot's clubs and associations and small craft airports. This may provide an avenue for finding a pilot who, for a few dollars, will take you and your son up in the air for 30 minutes or so.

There are also businesses that offer sightseeing tours on helicopters that last from 20 minutes to two hours. Commuter heliports for hops between airports or from downtown to the airport is another option. Imagine, if you will, going downtown, getting on a helicopter and flying to the airport. While at the airport have lunch. Then return via the bus or even a limousine. I'm sure you will do things according to your budget.

Live Chicken Dinner

One of my favorite activities is to take my sons to get their own food. This helps them to understand the reality of where meat comes from. We went to a live poultry shop, selected a chicken. It was de-feathered, butchered and cleaned for us. We took it home and cooked it.

There was a certain level of increased comprehension and satisfaction gained from this whole activity, from start to finish.

I suggest caution with how much of the butchering process you expose your young ones to - if at all. Use your judgement. You'll be surprised what questions will come up. They will know that chickens don't come from the grocery store or the refrigerator.

This activity also presents a good opportunity to grill or bar-b-que the chicken outdoors.

Breakfast
on the Beach

With good weather in mind Breakfast on the Beach can be a lot of fun. Pack a breakfast of your choice and a blanket. Head out to the beach early in the morning. If you're really ambitious get there before sunrise. Have breakfast with the morning waves. This is a good way to start a long day at the beach or just have breakfast and head back to your activities for the day. Plan ahead, you might fix breakfast, pack it up or pick up breakfast from a fast food place on your way to the beach. This can also be done for lunch or dinner.

This is a good time to just talk about life and the waves. If that's not enough, start counting the sand and see where that leads.

Let's go to the Movie

How many times have you had fried chicken in the movies? Tell the truth. I've had it many times and it is always fantastic to be watching a good movie, eating chicken and licking my fingers. Just fix the chicken (or buy from the local chicken joint on the way), take some paper plates and napkins, get some drinks and be on your way. Right after the movie starts serve up the meal and watch in style.

Note: some theaters don't allow you to take food into the movie - in that case buy hot-dogs.

In fact, that's a great surprise on a Saturday or Sunday afternoon. Ask your son if he would like a hot-dog - after he says yes you just whisk him off to the movie without even a warning. He won't realize what's going on until you turn into the driveway to the movie parking lot. Kids love surprises - good one's that is.

This surprise takes planning so that you can coordinate the timing to get there in plenty of time before the movie starts.

Do You Have a Relationship With God?

The Bible tells us that:

> *... **if you confess with your mouth, "Jesus is Lord," and believe in your heart that God raised him from the dead, you will be saved.***

Romans 10:9 KJV

HAVE YOU ACCEPTED JESUS AS YOUR LORD?

If you do not have a relationship with God – through accepting Jesus as Lord – then I invite you to please pray the following prayer:

> *Lord, I come before you today to confess that I accept Jesus as my Lord and Savior and that I believe you raised Him from the dead. I believe that He died for my sins and that only through Him can I be saved.*
>
> *Lord, please forgive me of all my sins and accept me into your Kingdom. Lord, I welcome the Holy Spirit into my heart today.*
>
> *I thank you, Lord, in Jesus' Name, Amen.*

Congratulations! Now, you - as a born-again Christian can best maintain your walk with God by:

- Praying daily – ask God to help you with the challenges in your life and to bring you closer to Himself
- Read and Study God's Word (the Bible) daily
- Attend a Bible teaching church
- Fellowship with other serious Christians

A good place to start your Bible reading is with the book of John.

If you have questions or need help please write to me at:

Akili Kumasi, **GOD IS LOVE MINISTRIES**
P.O. Box 80275, Brooklyn, NY 11208
kumasi@GILpublications.com

GOD IS LOVE

Mail Order ....GIL Publications
P. O. Box 80275, Brooklyn, NY 11208
Telephone Orders................(718) 386-6434
Website Orders ....www.GILpublications.com

SCRIPTURE REFERENCE BOOKS			
Book Title	**Price**	**#**	**Total**
God's Healing Scriptures 240 Prayers & Promises in the Bible	$9.95		
101 Women in the Bible	$6.95		
101 Prayers in the Bible	$6.95		
101 Victories in the Bible	$6.95		
HALL OF FAITH CLASSICS			
Volume 1: The Person and Work of the Holy Spirit (R.A. Torrey)	$9.75		
Volume 2: How to Pray (R.A. Torrey)	$5.95		
Volume 3: How To Obtain the Fullness of Power for Life and Christian Service (R.A. Torrey)	$5.75		
Volume 4: Absolute Surrender (Andrew Murray)	$6.25		
Volume 5: Humility: The Beauty of Holiness (Andrew Murray)	$5.75		
Hall of Faith 5-Pack (Volumes 1, 2, 3, 4, 5) - $25% off – Save $8.35	$25.10		
FATHERHOOD BOOKS			
Fatherhood Principles of Joseph the Carpenter	$8.95		
Fun Meals for Fathers and Sons	$4.95		
On the Outside Looking In	$7.95		

To pay by Credit / Debit Card – go to www.GILpublications.com or call 718-386-6434

Complete the Order Form on the next page

Mail Order .... GIL Publications
P. O. Box 80275, Brooklyn, NY 11208
Telephone Orders .... (718) 386-6434
Website Orders .... www.GILpublications.com

Book Title	Price	#	Total
Bible Word Search – Puzzles with Scriptures (80 puzzles per book)			
Vol. I: **Extracts** from the Bible	$7.95		
Vol. II: **Women** in the Bible	$7.95		
Vol. III: **Fathers** in the Bible	$7.95		
Vol. IV: **Prayers** in the Bible	$7.95		
Vol. V: **Victories** in the Bible	$7.95		
Vol. VI: **Parables** in the Bible	$7.95		
Vol. VII: **Promises** in the Bible	$7.95		
Vol. VIII: **Foundations** in Christianity (**100 Puzzles**)	$8.95		
Bible Word Search 8-Pack (all 8 books) *- 17% off – Save $11.00*	$53.62		
Bible Word Search, **Large Print, No. 1**	$5.95		
Church Edition CD - *560 puzzles* – (7 volumes, lesson plans, group activities)	$5.95		
EDUCATOR'S WORD SEARCH Vol. 1: U.S. Presidents	$5.95		
	Sub-Total		
	NY Residents Add 8.5% Tax		
	Shipping ($3.95 1st item, 50¢ each additional)		
	TOTAL		

Date:_____ Payment: ☑ Check ☑ Money Order

Name:_____

Address:_____

City:_____ State:_____ Zip:_____

Telephone:_____

E-Mail:_____